# THE PROMISE

*To Shanell
Peace and Blessings!
I wish all things wonderful for you and your work!!*

*Kent Cosby*

# THE
# PROMISE

*Poems of Reflection, Motivation and Peace*

Robert Cosby

Copyright © 2016 by Robert Cosby.

Library of Congress Control Number:   2016917283
ISBN:         Hardcover            978-1-5245-5220-6
              Softcover            978-1-5245-5221-3
              eBook                978-1-5245-5222-0

All rights reserved. No part of this book may be reproduced or transmitted in any form or by any means, electronic or mechanical, including photocopying, recording, or by any information storage and retrieval system, without permission in writing from the copyright owner.

This is a work of fiction. Names, characters, places and incidents either are the product of the author's imagination or are used fictitiously, and any resemblance to any actual persons, living or dead, events, or locales is entirely coincidental.

Any people depicted in stock imagery provided by Thinkstock are models, and such images are being used for illustrative purposes only.
Certain stock imagery © Thinkstock.

Print information available on the last page.

Rev. date: 10/20/2016

To order additional copies of this book, contact:
Xlibris
1-888-795-4274
www.Xlibris.com
Orders@Xlibris.com
686376

# CONTENTS

Acknowledgements .................................................................. vii
Find Me .................................................................................. 1
Rhema ................................................................................... 2
Reckoning .............................................................................. 3
Invincible ............................................................................... 4
Divining My Future ................................................................ 5
Latticeworks of Iron .............................................................. 6
Promise .................................................................................. 8
Mother and Son ..................................................................... 9
Family Secrets ...................................................................... 10
Bleeding Hearts .................................................................... 11
Guardian Angel .................................................................... 12
Fast Shoes ............................................................................ 14
Water Balloons .................................................................... 15
Mianus River ........................................................................ 16
Factory Workers .................................................................. 19
Flags ..................................................................................... 20
Main Street .......................................................................... 21
Pomp and Circumstance ...................................................... 22
Pillow ................................................................................... 24
Bamboo and Sunlight .......................................................... 25
Mountain Lake View ............................................................ 26
Bear Pit ................................................................................ 27

| | |
|---|---|
| Running out of Town | 28 |
| Colors | 29 |
| Asylum | 31 |
| Drink of Water | 32 |
| The Swing | 34 |
| Nine Angels | 36 |
| A Child's Laughter | 37 |
| Laying on of Hands | 38 |
| Music Stories | 40 |
| Post-Communion Buzz | 42 |
| Not Knowing Beauty | 43 |
| Breathing | 45 |
| Max and Me | 46 |
| The Thrill Is Gone | 47 |
| Morning (For My Father) | 48 |
| Times Square | 50 |
| Forgiveness | 51 |
| Change | 52 |
| Care Full | 53 |
| As It Should Be | 54 |
| Promised Land | 55 |
| Index | 57 |
| Photographs— In Order They Appear | 59 |

# Acknowledgements

**My Compass Points**

Chris Llewellyn deserves particular thanks for her interest in the author's work and her friendship. The Takoma Park Poetry Group too provided support and perceptive comment.

Also, thanks to David Todd for his critical assessment and to Annie and Bob Brown, David Cato, and the Ascension Church family.

Special appreciation goes to Anne Becker for her perceptive reading and editing and to Lendeh Sherman, whose technical assistance, cover design, and layout expertise were invaluable. Consultants Lyca Sinclair and Christine Lapas and their Xlibris publishing team.

The greatest appreciation is reserved for my wife, Leona and family, especially the author's sister, Renata Cosby, for her significant contribution. Her criticism, suggestions, and editing were founded on her belief and confidence in the author's talent.

A special thank-you is also extended to my brother-in-law Michael McMahon.

And that is the essence of the matter. The author is grateful to all those who believe in him and in the power of poetry that continues to give him voice and direction.

# Find Me

where lightning strikes
thrown down from heaven
this is where I wait for you
electric air
smell of power
pulled down from the sky
spread across ocean
complete and instantaneous
like a promise

# Rhema

a homeless person, I shake
shiver not from cold
but from grief
the living word, the thing said
Logos and Dabar
set in motion
pray, ask for blessings
to soothe, to touch
love by itself
a quiet place to listen

brain and heart fused
thinking, hearing, sensing
uttered words free me
loosed soul rises
with the blessing words provide
filled with light
with gratitude

# Reckoning

get on with your life they said
Hail Mary
find out what was done
full of grace
she said it was sad he was
rewarded for bad behavior

why was no one defrocked?
blessed are you who take the opportunity to change
can he be forgiven?
I look people in the face seeing the worry lines
smile sadly
knowing their anger and pain

documents show he was moved not removed
who deserved to be rewarded for bad behavior?
was I so bad he punished me?
angry they are free
children's shoes like mine still remind me
of the bodies that filled them

pray for us sinners

they said their compulsions were cured by God
covered up like holy cloth in tunic and breastplate
wondering when did God say that was okay?
waiting for the reckoning and salvation
now and at the hour of our death

# Invincible

the Sirens softly beckon
I am as a sailor rowing with Odysseus
moaning waves lift and carry me
our vessel's drumbeats fill the air
my oar strokes deep and strong
I seek treasures of antiquity
dreams hidden and found
you are my courageous captain

prone to anger because I am afraid
there are holes in the ocean and in me I cannot see
we row on, pulsating rhythms pound out our time
Smooth waters ahead, I dream of galaxies unexplored
you, father, have shaped me
I awaken know you are there
together we are strong

# Divining My Future

if I could divine my future
I find just the spot
intersection of homes and dreams
tried-and-true place of hard work
following the narrow path where others diverge
I would raise the rod and watch it quiver
see the field in the sky where the sun casts shadows

among fields of broken earth and dry grass
come to the place just right
where I'd hear my grandmother say, "reward yourself
every now and again for your work"

I would plunge a marker in the ground
where the forked rod quivered
and smile because Big Ma would say
"I do declare that is God's work
filled with prayer and sweat"

I wonder how many rainmakers went before
knowing the earth and sky give what they will

growing old
impatient for answers
I imagine my petitions float high in heaven
with rapt concentration
crossed rod outstretched
my face tilted skyward like a child watching snowfall
feeling the earth below
arms wide, alone in the field
I stand
where I know water is

# Latticeworks of Iron

dawn drops frost that glistens
your beauty around me a phosphorescent scaffolding
intricately I build my love
strong bonds held with welded rivets

just enough words hold my love
frozen as in glass blocks, pure ice
each word freighted and free
words carefully defrosted, a nectar tasted

I want to savor your voice
feel the timbre
hold what you say
delicate lattice
work of words

gathered like abandoned railroad ties
build trestles in my mind
each deep red word holds heat within
apart they are frozen slivers avoided as broken glass

tantalizing white shards float in the sky and land on your lashes
words of love shroud and clothe the trees
translucent alabaster coats
warm me in the forest of winter

take hold of me and touch my soul
come meet me where I wait
by the iron trestle that crosses
the wild river to my heart

# Promise

where the whelming flood drowns me
my own story
my experiences
my struggles thrown down like an anchor
the liberty you provide each day
to see darkness and glimpses of light
a gift of hope brought into sharp focus
you offer me the whole staircase of faith
if only I take the first step by itself
walking down the road seeing your footsteps in snow
carrying the torch you gave me
it is my time to be courageous
to know a truth within

# Mother and Son

you sit at the bench to play
I climb with little legs to kneel
then sit beside you
I listen
I am learning to read you
to see your light

music sounds in the air
my heart lights with the harmony and crescendos
notes raised to the roof reflect light,
entering and exiting stained glass prisms
you, my mother, you smile with me

the same mother who tends me when I'm sick
scolds me when I'm wrong, taught me to stand strong
feeds me with the milk of the spirit
shows me how to live amid rocks
and find the stepping-stones of life

now you are old and I sit with you
holding hands, feeling your power, seeing you smile
giving thanks

# Family Secrets

don't ask for too much
'cause you won't get it anyway
don't tell anyone anything about yourself
it will only be used against you
I learned this from my family

preworrying like a pessimist
I worry I am a worrier
trying to be transparent
how many things I was told made good sense?

can defensive layers be peeled back
like worn onion skin?
can decisions be made with joy?
can my inner voice prevail
and talk to those I love?

when can I tell my story?

each sound falling down from the sky
can I be hurt and still offer help?
am I a coin to be spent?
do I wait to hurt so good?

my cup almost empty
still it is running over

now I tell my story

# Bleeding Hearts

Mom looked down
where her bleeding hearts matured
she grew rainbows of flowers
bunches of life pushing forth from fertile rocky soil
my village filled with driveways of satisfaction
prideful male owners of Dodge Darts, Plymouth Furys,
    Chevys, and Fords
mothers piloted sedans and station wagons like commuter
    boats with kids peering out

crocuses signaled the awakening of spring
the smell of burned leaves from neighbors' yards hung in the air
faded memories of *LIFE* magazine pictures of jungles far away
where sky and vegetation painted orange
lit by napalm's jellied liquid raining down
as dark metal birds disappeared above
pictures of bodies running like souls escaping hell's rising flames

Civil Rights protests and exaggerated numbers of Vietcong killed
awkward teen moments raking and wading through piles of wet
    oak leaves that would not burn
"get the can" is all Father said
I peered into the opening of red liquid
then poured the vaporous fluid
too many leaves soaked as if from a fountain
Dad glared at me

the earthy and pungent odor of rotting foliage
mingled with gasoline vapors
another day in the scrapbook of memories I wanted to burn
lit with Mom's stainless steel lighter
the one just like James Dean used when smoking was cool
now rich loam dropped on her metal container of ashes
just past the bleeding heart bush with its pink-and-white blossoms
its green branches holding little hearts not yet open

# Guardian Angel

I smiled when Mom brought you home
I watched you as you grew
your chubby face reddened every time you cried
waving arms and kicking legs
enjoying the world around you

you would smile
often
hands delicate
fingernails like flower buds
I touched your fingers to mine,
and we both laughed

as big brother, I vowed to protect you
I was your guardian angel
my wings covered you lest you dash your foot against a stone
as a child you loved fireworks
we craned our necks toward the heavens to see the bombs bursting in air

a gangbanger's stray bullet found you
I looked down to see you fallen
I thought you were dead
you said your feet were free
looking up at me
gone numb like going to the dentist
"I failed to protect you"
I cried

years later, we cry and laugh together
as I look at your strong arms
gripping your gleaming black metal chair
you tell me I am still your guardian angel
and you are mine

# Fast Shoes

when I was young, I wanted neat shoes
mother made me wear sharkskin-reinforced round-toed shoes
as I grew, I wanted cool shoes like the grown ups
I would settle for Hush Puppies, not the food but the shoes

smart suede shoes like the cool cats wore
as a teen, I wanted boots, desert boots, Beatle boots,
    hiking boots, biker boots
stompin' boots to match the look on my face
what I really wanted was fast shoes

faster than PF Flyers, Converse All Stars, Tigers
and Adidastars, Nike Jordans sure would look cool
run like the wind and jump to the sky
I coveted fast shoes, spiked shoes
hurtin' shoes all the same

spiked ones could run you down
make you bleed shoes jump and hurdle barriers
racing shoes, jets for the feet, rocket propelled
magic shoes spoke my name, knew I could run like the Flash

rainbow shoes, splashed with color
just lace them up, take them for a spin
shoes that meant business
shoes knew their purpose
as soon as you took your first strides

molded to your feet, shoes that brought smiles to your face
brought you to your knees at the end of the race
bruised, blackened, bleeding, and triumphant
triumphant, yeah,
I want fast shoes

# Water Balloons

springtime drenched me with shades of green and yellow
flowers offer life—the promise of youth
afternoon classes cancelled
sunny day warm in the April light
a cool breeze blowing daffodils
impetuous, testing boundaries full of hormones and ideas

this brash group of acned adolescents talking fast
laughing with the bag of mischief balloons
each teen had a job to do on the assembly line
stretching and placing the balloon mouth on the spigot
I tied off and stashed each one by size like ordinance
demarcation lines of friend and foe still fuzzy between us
wondered if every person for themselves
was true of water wars and friendships

before emerging into bright spring light
overflowing with possibilities
dragging the plastic garbage bag down dimly lit hallways
laughing as if we were mad
contemplating which dorm rooms to throw from
anticipating the looks on the faces of the doused
rite of passage, a kind of ecstasy

# Mianus River

ice layers move and stop on the Connecticut riverbed at low tide
serpentine trickles of water dance on the mud and ice around the
    dredged channel
abandoned finger paintings anchored white channel floats with brown
    watermarks gather
seaweed hair attached to mooring ropes on bobbing buoys,
    red moons signal deep water

tethered lines hold fast to the shore
blue-gray ice sheets, dull, opaque, show off edges that sparkle in late
    afternoon sun
escaping air sounds of the bubbler near shore, keep boats from being
    ice bound against the pier
larger shards heave and shift, crack and creak in the cold

pulled apart by the river moon, pale frozen panels appear as if broken-
    winged fallen angels stir below
bulrushes bend and straighten in the wind; someone making way on a
    run to the sea
wheat, green and rust colored, sea grasses lie down in clumps
black ooze hides secrets under the ice; the rail bridge tower looms in
    the distance where they used to dive at high tide brave and foolish,
    they yelled, "better dead than crippled"
diving fists first, those projectiles accelerating their bodies in a rush to
    disappear under the river's face
dinghies dragged high on rocky shores lean over, forgotten toys

large pleasure craft lay, beached whales sleeping
we laughed at first then anxiously yelled obscenities
staring at the emerging bubbles
eyes wide, "stop foolin around"

sailboats next to floating docks, furled sails, once full, now stowed
    neatly below
tucked in for winter's slumber, plastic sheathing covers them
"stop foolin around" echoes and howls, voices of the Northeast wind

high tides, boating joy and haunting acts linger

recollections of courage, wholeness, and sophomoric zeal
rest like sound channel markers
probing and searching again and again for the connection
rework cherished summers on the Mianus, all fade over time

his mother refuses to let him go
secrets whispered below the river surface
where swift currents flow
the sea tide's tendrilled fingers
taking what the Mianus gives willingly
submerged and free, feelings on currents moving quietly out to sea

# Factory Workers

I wanted my world to be bigger
so I would not feel trapped
as a teen, I stared at the buildings nearby
with blackened windows bolted shut

In good weather, I watched the workers at lunchtime
bodies streamed out of the shops
young and old faces with the same look
greasy lunch bags and pails held mechanically, lovingly, or with disdain
each crossed the street like Styx to moments of semi-freedom
a temporary favorite space in the grass, at picnic tables
others leaned against the fence by the ball field back stop

steady hands carefully poured precious liquids from metal
    containers into cups
tired eyes watched the progress of boccie games
thin men holding lighted cigs offered racy, raunchy comments,
in languages I didn't understand

others with blank expressions stared
except for unkept promises, nothing inside
each appeared to hang on
black eyes in dull skin
and at the appointed time, they shuffled back inside

I should have listened to their unspoken words

# Flags

stars and stripes luft in the wind
rising and falling to a blowing rhythm
symbol of freedom most take for granted
freedom is not free

stone monuments to people and places
fill the landscape, memories to hearts broken in exchange for victories
heroes etched in black and white
where no one questions toughness

spirits in the clouds whisper shhh, shhh
blue skies with floating white beards
come and see us they implore
sparkling water ripples on the river

sunlight glistens on droplets
that mirror the sun
white caps lay on the waves, each keep beat
with lapping sounds, squish, lop, squish, lop
in the distance
trees of life and more tributes to the fallen

geese fly by, land on polo fields now abandoned
whirling bird blades overhead
jets speed to destinations far and wide
their sounds roar in the blue yonder

crisp air and traffic sounds in the near distance
museums of stone and glass collect memories and artifacts
teach beauty and culture
Holocaust, money, and books
children's bodies filled with promise, their voices bright

each a future that unfolds, maps that are hard to read
flags rise now fully unfurled
circling the monument, snapping and blowing in the wind

# Main Street

my street, my America
filled with shops and storefront sidewalk sales in summer
now blankets of snow warm the toes of trees in the town square
friends whisper of experiences of survival
put on a positive face they shape every morning in the mirror

relatives come like deer in the woods to eat and run
darting from the serious troubles no one wants to hear
think of familial bonds like maple roots spreading as their fingers in the ground
they pass in front of buildings once important
car dealerships now vacant

clapboard, brick, and stone ajar
historic houses' names of special families stand sentry
people shared meals and language here
all you can eat
pancake breakfasts at rectangular tables held in church halls and lodges

those that cannot pay are still invited
religious icons share the street
God's hot meals, simple repasts
serve as respite
distractions from a harsh reality like winds of change

folks settle down here with family, friends, feel secure
high schoolers cruise the main drag to see and be seen
in American cars and trucks, telephone poles
measure the distance to fields, woods, highways out of town
signs blow in the wind

still winter's grip holds on, spruced up with sunshine and blue skies
bundled bodies with turned-up collars and wind-burned faces
Kiwanis, Lions, Rotary Club members now older still appraise
life on Main Street
tree branches, rusted signs slowly sway
in the wind

# Pomp and Circumstance

the sky shines pulsating watercolors
deep blue with dollops of white brushstroke
clouds float silently as far as eye can see
marsh grasses, brown and green, fill with water and the living
briny branches, tendrils of undulating fingers

in the distance, the hushed sun plans its entrance
horizon's vibrant strata: orange, gray, white, lavender
color layered another on another on another
gives way to golden aura, pomp and circumstance
of the coming morning sun

# Pillow

holder of my dreams
awakens with me in the morning
the lament of the dove
cuts through the cool spring air
my pillow indented where my head laid

filled with imaginings, with sentences unfinished,
and spittle comatose bliss had lain
my companion has been beaten
thrown about as a stunt double on a mystery set

cotton, rayon, and down filled ticking inside
hold a maze of memories, imprisoned dreams
thoughts bound in the darkness
I try to catch each one, counting sheep,

elusive, private riddles, enigmas, and love tragedies often leave my
    eyes wide
my waiting pillow quiet as a holding cell
my silent *consigliere* advises me
"just rest your weary head here for a while and sleep"

"I will help you if you allow me" the pillow implores
I slumber and awaken refreshed today
forgetting I am the troubled prisoner unsure of tomorrow
my pillow holds the stories like Scheherazade
waiting to weave a new dream

# Bamboo and Sunlight

life lifts skyward, leaves unfurl
sunlight greets the tops of bamboo leaves caressing the sky
growing, always growing to the heavens
I incline my eyes to see your glory
O lover of light

I lie in your leaves
between your shadowed limbs and listen
I inhale your scent
stalks of green, thick and growing
each one thrusts higher, arches to the clouds

sun bathes by the sea
sunlight bright and piercing reaches each shoot and spear
spears touch the sky
tall and strong, undulating in the breeze
leaves unfold and bask
wind helps them sing

# Mountain Lake View

the sky's gray lens diffuse the sunlight
shrouded trees cast shadows black on white, like photographic plates
fog rolls in to cover the mountainous landscape
the shoreline surreal, a painting glazed with dull mist
boats seem to float in the sky

the water and sky merge
the setting sun momentarily peeks through
beauty unleashed in the distance
buzzing bees search for blossoms
to cavort in and leave like Casanovas
the smell of water and marsh arrest the senses

like seeing my childhood home
felled trees line the woods
logs strewn like bowling pins on angular terrain
older trees with rings signifying their years of marriage with the earth
memories recorded each year
years of hard and long winters
years of bounty

passages of chapters
separation of fertile earth and air
manicured shores that reflect the temperament of the community
the knurled plane trees grow
pushed and pulled
ducks gather and dance in the water

short trunks and closely cut branches look like an ogre's scepters
waiting for battle
my jumbled thoughts begin to crystallize as I see my reflection
water turns from gray to deep blue to blend with the sky
the sun burns off the vapor
I can see clearly
how pressure changes our family landscape
in the distance, trees fade from view

# Bear Pit

on the banks of a river they hide
camouflaged, angry, and afraid
wishing for a chance to see the sky
without walls

sunshine and crisp air are expected to be enough
concrete pits confine and constrict

keepers improve their space
tributary banks of trees, shrubs to hold the soil
outcroppings of boulders

living water runs cold to drink
I see their eyes, sacred places
where spirit lives unfold

remember acts of love and hate,
their faces reflect in pools and eddies
do they recognize themselves?
do they see a way to cross river to mountains

scented flowers cover the ground
evergreens shade the rocks
wherever sun shines and land unfolds
they remember mother's milk, honey
what it means to be free

# Running out of Town

The workers filled the last crates, arks hermetically sealed
the contents labeled "bone boxes"
fragments of history
close your eyes and imagine a journey
traveling back through time, back of thousands of millennia

to a pasture of rich green and yellow leaves and stalks
in a valley of sunshine
earthy smells
rotting vegetation permeates the hot steamy air
smells of huge bodies of living creatures waft in the gentle breeze
blue-brown mountains shine in the distance like gems

birds screech a welcome or a warning, then gigantic silence

standing motionless for a moment near a stand of trees
stomach gurgling, long strings of saliva drip from his mouth
rows of teeth like huge daggers appear as the mouth opens
menacing red eyes peer down, staring at lunch

terrifyingly glorious behemoth of the valley
legs spring forward, surprisingly nimble for the massive body
bounding now like a giant dog with an enormous head chasing down a
    huge-horned rabbit
we could be that rabbit

the semi tractor-trailer doors close
boxes safely inside
this town overlooks the same valley
an ancient burial ground
small bodies devour the immense

the driver and semi pull out of town
turn the corner, rolling faster
headed to the interstate
boxes destined for feeding eyes
hungry museum minds, thousands of miles away
the *T. rex* bound for glory

# Colors

natives, we are of the same mother
we were once immigrants, slaves of the middle passage
we work the fields, gather fabric, sew, and thresh
we eat these foods of our people, corn, maize, hominy,
    and buckwheat, blue, white, yellow, and red
we remember grandmothers and mothers preparing the
    meals we cherished

foods sprinkled with laughter, and celebratory foods filled with our own
    ancestors
those that fought for and died
for water, hunting and voting rights, for freedoms we take for granted

brothers and sisters of muted yellow, burnt umber, Jordan brown,
    indigo red, and ebony black
we mix and match our lives, our skins
an artist's palette
so our colors are different, reddened skin,
café au lait, light brown and tan, even titanium whites

pay attention, and it might transform how you see me
we are a collection of storied people
we share scars as oppressors and oppressed

We all break bread together
each mouthful of corn pudding, rice cake, flatbread, corn bread,
    tortilla, beans, and pies
*take me home*
*through memories*

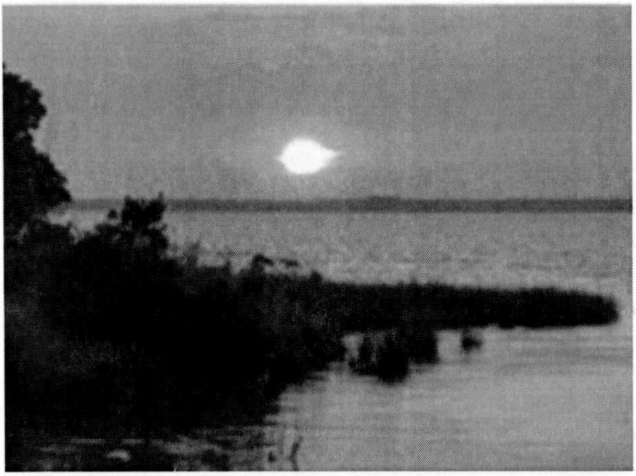

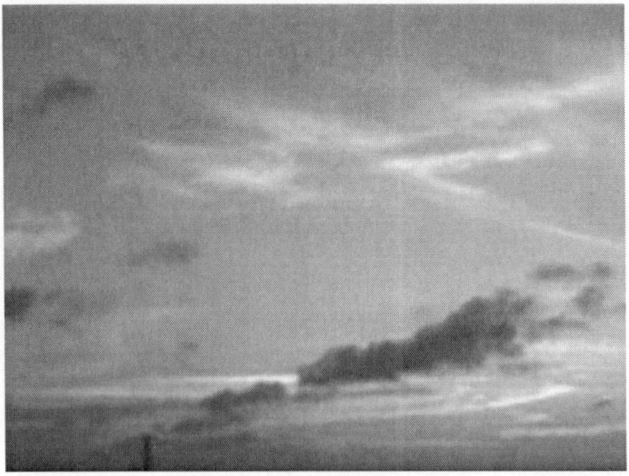

# Asylum

an asylum seeker looking for a better life
I apply and wait, pass the time learning the things seen and unseen

avoided on the street like a detour sign
I am unclean despite my daily washing
my voice is hoarse from wailing

they want my story
they judge with hmms and harrumphs
I record for them my descent into hell

I cannot escape feeling a victim
my mother watched me run and hide
she left me, abandoned

so you might find me
and I smile so I will be more worthy
I grovel for handouts, to work, to smooth the sand

I recognize the irony of righteousness and mercy
they live both together and apart like feuding lovers
for my life, I ask of them both

a child warrior, despicable, entrusted to the care of strangers
I ask for forgiveness
a fallen angel, absolved

# Drink of Water

is the water good?
the parched earth is cracked and broken
riverbeds, rocky streams once gurgling
free and singing, now dry

can there be enough clean water?
now I am thirsty for a long, cold swallow
greedy for plenty to bathe and frolic in
the joy of the spring-fed lake, our favorite watering hole
where we skinny-dipped and found our vigor

we seek to impose our will on events
rubbing hard with puffed-out chests
wizards conjuring water out of a bottle

heads tilted skyward like turkeys
waiting for the rain

in my own vision
I saw little boys pleading for a drink of water
licking dry lips until the black radiated rain poured down
no one gave them a sip before they died
dismissed as collateral damage,
discarded in the name of good intentions,
and industrial might called progress
and still the sun rises
beating out the day's rhythms

we hope for a fertile spring of farmer's rain soaking in
the scythe waits for a dwindling harvest, the heat pours down, no relief
I stand looking at the fractured ground

I stand in the garden of good and evil
thinking I have the answer for the drought
taste pure water
so cleansing it takes my breath away

I pray a spirit will come down,
grant us mercy, grant us rain

"And it shall come to pass afterward,
that I will pour out my Spirit on all flesh;
your sons and your daughters shall prophesy,
your old men shall dream dreams,
and your young men shall see visions"(Joel 2:28).

# The Swing

my daughter climbs
I watch, seated on a bench
she swings free on the monkey bars

the other children, blond-
and brown-haired little girls scream
"go home, black bitch"
shocked

shocked, as if spat upon, I am paralyzed for an instant,
my daughter undaunted, drops to the ground
she demands "why are they so mean?"

I stand to offer comfort
her face calm, unfazed
my grandmother's strength in her eyes

"push me on the tire swing"
I oblige, my eyes filled with tears
my heart branded like chattel

those that teach their children to hate
in the distance now staring back
they wonder what comes next

darkness grows like thunderheads
I heard they sang songs
and laughed running down the church stairs

absence of sound follows as smoke clears
rubble covered braids and ribboned pigtails in Birmingham
and light beams down, angels are rising

slingshot and arrowed words
still find their mark
I want to be strong, not dwell on the past
my fears and hopes, like the dream, perhaps forgot

memories still wanting a pound of flesh
needing justice, forgiveness, and salvation
swing low as the spiritual moves

my tears gather like rainwater to irrigate trees bearing strange fruit
the playground tire swings in lazy arcs

silence chases the birds
little girls gone too
my daughter directs me home

# Nine Angels

nine lives snuffed out no longer share their light
senseless pain triggered
because one hates, I mourn

we assemble, kneel in huddled masses
because you said You would be there
whenever two or more gather
walk with us, carry me

when again, we come to this stop on the underground railroad
heal us, focus us, bring our voices together
to sing of joy, sing of pain
seeing angels shield us with their wings
heal our hearts, watch us

nine more angels now fly free
And my dreams of forgiveness come in the night
because love and enduring justice start with Thee

# A Child's Laughter

laughter contagious starts with a tingling in the ears
laughter so fresh you forget all but the moment
children's laughter balm and magic elixir

smiles guiltless and simple
a guffaw sneaks up slowly stealthily
then crashes like a wave at the shore
surprised, submerged, rises breathless

laughing children whisper in one another's ears
followed by rolling laughter
joy bubbles, overflows revealing
innocence
treasured gold

unwrapped like candy
I savor the sounds
when I see
the picture of you

# Laying on of Hands

sister power grabs me
moves on in silence, with a nod
cupped in secret word and clapped in song
vital hands and strong arms
on the shoulders of those that went before
hands teaching others the meaning of
love greater than measure
greet me, like a grandmother's wisdom

a sista's love offers a furyand compassion as great
hands that offer the heart
compassion that spreads in ripples
smoothing troubled waters

hands that smell sweet feel soft
offer the touch of understanding
the heat of other sun's rays
warm the palms and backs of working hands
magic-reaching hands

work at night when the moon's beams wash over their skin
hands that bring a baby into the world
offer aid or tender caress
clasping hands together hold power
pray for who departs this life

powerful hands hold the electricity of the moment
healing hands carry the power of the spirit
the quiet urgency of a mother
comforting her child
hands carry power
aid the brokenhearted, the discouraged, the sick
hands touch in the silence of caring

hands with spots that pat and hold fast
hands cover faces filled with cleansing tears
these hands ask for miracles
chubby and bony, elegant and rough, held together asking for divine help
these hands that hold the bond of sisters
sisterhood, yes, sisterhood that lay on hands of sisters

# Music Stories

melodies stuck in my head
notes rising and falling
small boats on a large sea
rhythmic paths, colorful strokes
major and minor chords
expressed in harmony and downbeat beauty

telling stories of love and laughter
faith despite doubt
atonal lifetime signatures
jagged and painful like stepping on glass
feeling the classic hurt, I love just because
it sounds so beautiful I want to cry

women and men in sweatshops and brothels, hospitals and schools
working, surviving, shining, carrying on
music sees them through
sultry hips swaying and swinging to a soulful beat
strutting proud, stompin' with gospel rhythms

music takes them to a place
where hurt is forgotten
like a new morning's light
sweetness like love flowing lingers
a heartfelt pounding in their ears and veins
hope takes wing, it flies
to those that need

remember that dancing in the dark
a feathery touch, a bump and grind
seduced and seducer, the phrasing,
the bars and stanzas on a line like
warm breath
on ears, skin touching skin
invisible notes raised by translucent music

men and women cheatin' and drinkin'
cryin' and laughin, lovin' and fightin'
ballads of love, you resist as long as you can
backdoor lovers, best friends gone bad
drumbeats, downbeats, fortissimo, pianissimo, adagio, and rest

kisses melting as they spread
loving kindness and savage expression
aphrodisiac and call to battle, music
beautiful sorrow at night
sweet surrender, in the coming light
O sweet surrender, joy moving in the mornin'

# Post-Communion Buzz

in morning light, magnificent ribbons of light
the prayer at my lips is for the pain bearer
braids of compassion surround me
dreadlocks of comfort and solace

when silence drowns me
fill me with mustard seeds of faith
to listen as grasses and flowers turning to the sun
that seal me
settle me

I come again to be fed and restored by the cup
my communion buzz, surrogate spirit
wine of life that arrests and intoxicates the senses
fill me as full as the breath I breathe

drown me in love,
where righteousness and peace
kiss the sky
help me seek the clarity of truth
hasten my understanding
take my breath away

# Not Knowing Beauty

you captured me
your walk
your eyes sparkling clear
remembering how you gazed at the night sky
the stars winking as iridescent diamonds
untainted and without blemish

a sultry confidence unrepentant and unlearned
vibrant and floating
your reservoir of love overflowing

take me with you to that place
where time waits and you walk unhurried
know each moment, reflection of light
bobbing on the sea

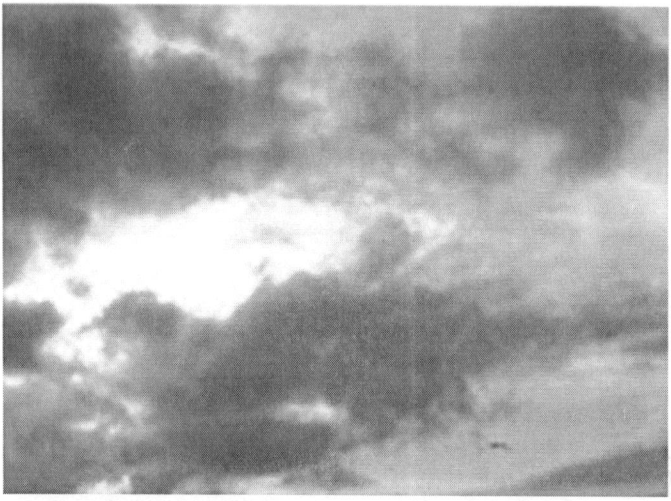

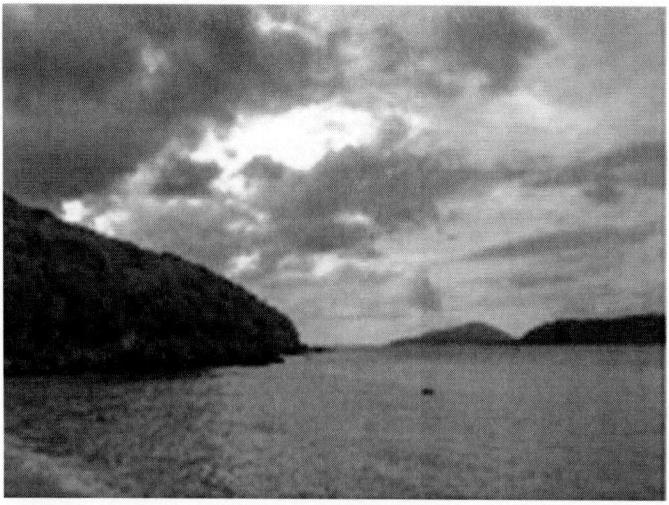

# Breathing

your light shines from above
warm breath surrounds me
golden rays lightly touch
a dove descends gliding
you fill me with grace

music dances in the air
I want to see you again full of life
you tell me you are always here
I can only see a hole of missing earth

watch me shovel the snow
being there with me
waiting with me patiently for spring
tell me where to plant the flowers

teach me to recognize essentials
to inhale the essence
the moment when everything changes
when your breath fills me

# Max and Me

he lays there quietly, peering at the door
his posture relaxed yet coiled
ready to leap into action
at dusk, the birds call
and sing in golden light
he sees me

jumps to attention
then slowly stretches front and back
he curbs his enthusiasm
subtle, slow circling
not to show his cards

but I see his tail
whirring like a helicopter blade
close to lift off
bleary eyed, I grab the leash
the tether, a formality

we open the door to enter the milky light
push open and
slip into sacred space

# The Thrill Is Gone

radio voices awaken me
each day, the same beginning
light brightens my room as the dawn breaks
today I hear the news
you have gone away

as a child I loved
hearing the blues that whined guitar riffs
you came into my home and talked to me welcoming me to your kingdom

your words told stories of loss and separation
loves gone bad
love that endured
your earhooks took me to another place
you shared your life as a hardworkin' Mississippi blues man

singin' of women, cheatin' and drinkin'
in a hurtin', lovin', stompin', humble, proud, and defiant sort of way
the blues done come down on me since you've gone
you have gone my star, you've gone
you and Lucille have gone away

the thrill is gone
the king is free

# Morning (For My Father)

beauty of the rising sun
nourished tulip blossoms to pop with color
birds converse about the day
a crow blares his caws about Momma
all bravado like the day is his
you are here too

the breeze passes
bringing a lightness of spirit
flowing across the space
reminding me of adolescence
gangly and awkward bodies
with new bumps and unruly hair

you said I would mature

majestic light now brings memories
of strength and experience
wisdom offered with kindness

you treated each day as special
overflowing with promise
and a radiant bright smile

filling me like the warmth of suns

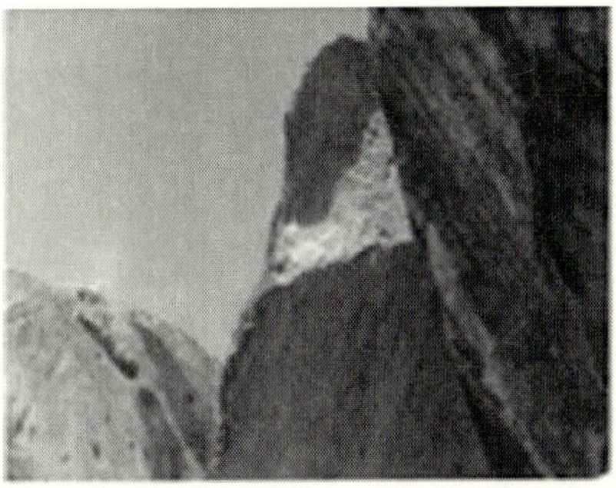

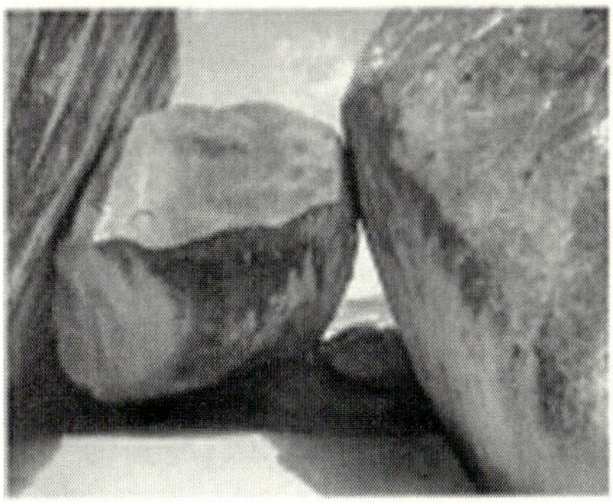

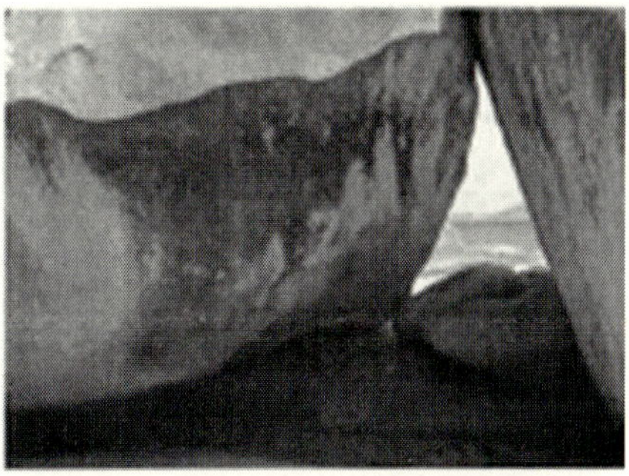

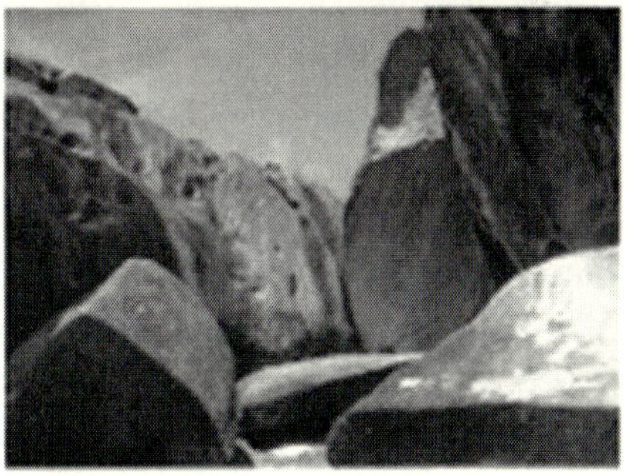

# Times Square

I took a commuter train to the city that never sleeps
the clickity-clack of steel wheels on rails rocking me to slumber
waking in a start to the conductor in dark blue
shepherding a throng of revelers
like teens eager to celebrate the moments
filled with the excitement and audacity of youth
I too follow, watching the hucksters on the streets
barking in earnest "check it out
pick a card, any card"

costumed adults hustling, selling and buying
asking "what are you looking for?"
the masses congregating like congealed gelatin
wanting to be part of humanity and history
sucking down cocktails of success
the exuberance of capitalism fêted
humored by love and kindness songs sung off-key
sharing for old times' sake a communion of fun and festivities
strangers forgetting the past caught up in the night

shuffling to keep warm
where the air is electric
waiting for the witching hour
swept into a magical and mysterious spell
where majestic moments with energy overflowing hold a certain truth
bound and wrapped like a present for expectant lovers caught in the
    moment
celebrating the coming New Year and all the possibilities
why am I here?
check my watch and hope to make the last train home

# Forgiveness

amber and rose morning skies
layered with gold tones
hang a rainbow on the horizon
in my ear, jangled chords of dissonance
why was I such a bonehead?

longing for strong sensations to well up
an intense euphoria close to pain
leading me, a dog on a leash

pulling me, pulling me faster and faster
until I resist, yanking back just before I fall
losing control and balance,

I finger a talisman paper clip in my pocket
to distract my fear and anger
why can't I listen to my own heart?

silence and solitude evade me
until I recall a song of my childhood
"this old man came rolling home"

"with a knickknack, paddy whack,"
tail wagging, the dog stands watching
I smile to remember: forgiveness
forgiveness starts inside the self

# Change

if I could change, I would change who am I in this moment
change the way I look at flowers
each petal precise and stunning

I would recognize the eyes of more people
look deeper with every encounter
listen more to music and look more at art

the opportunity to thank someone may not come again
if I could change, I would live each day with urgency
if I could change, I would hug more, learn more
I would smile, make each smile contagious
I would remember what makes me laugh

if I could change, I would worry less
about the slights, the slings,
the hurt of growing up and growing older

if I could change who I am in this moment
unburden my baggage, be wiser
revel in what it means to travel light

if I could change, I would breathe and stay in this moment
it will not come again

# Care Full

edges of years
careful not to forget
jagged ages

chances at a carnival booth
rings tossed into upright pins

each flying saucer slides through the air
out of balance like me
slightly off-kilter

years pass slowly at first
then accelerate
a train gathering speed
passing in twilight and into the night
clickity-clack the years pass
telephone poles in a barren landscape

tossed carefree, wobbling
teetering on the edge
laughing, spinning, and living

I catch the neck of the pin
hold on
like a Hula-Hoop I circle

knowing sometimes I miss the mark
my ring toss, my balance, my all
teetering careful
not to fall

# As It Should Be

when I was thirteen, the world was a dream
who would I be? who would I love?
eyes in the mirror, kind, the chin strong

compassionate cheekbones of my mother
eyebrows definitely your contribution
your hands larger than mine enveloped me

oh, how I tried to escape,
a smoldering teen, resenting if offered, every good suggestion
if I could recite Rudyard Kipling or Edna St. Vincent Millay
if I could be all the things you wanted me to
who would I become?

a strong monster, a good bum, a wise man, a gentle, loving giant
but could I be . . . no, not you, not you

you measured success with your ruler
how I wanted to calibrate my own

"temper the small successes with the failures"
I wondered would I ever be good enough

Now I look in the mirror again
I smile, laugh, content, at ease
I can only be myself
but still I hear your voice: "everything is as it should be"

# Promised Land

let me have the courage to walk in your footsteps
past the pulpits, past the altar rails
past hushed meeting rooms and upper chambers
help me see your presence in hotels, hospitals, hospices,
    boxes of the homeless,
stately mansions and homely houses
let me see you in the faces of those that I meet

let me forget the pain that comes with striving
let me smile with the grinning children and the old people who cackle
let me laugh and laugh at myself

let me remember how funny I look when I frown
help me not forget how I played in the dirt
may your strength be present when I am reluctant
let me remember that all things are possible
though the land we seek is not promised
nor getting there assured

# Index

**A**

As It Should Be  54
Asylum  31

**B**

Bamboo and Sunlight  25
Bear Pit  27
Bleeding Hearts  11
Breathing  45

**C**

Care Full  53
Change  52
A Child's Laughter  37
Colors  29

**D**

Divining My Future  5
Drink of Water  32

**F**

Factory Workers  19
Family Secrets  10
Fast Shoes  14
Find Me  1
Flags  20
Forgiveness  51

**G**

Guardian Angel  12

**I**

Invincible  4

**L**

Latticeworks of Iron  6
Laying on of Hands  38

**M**

Main Street  21
Max and Me  46
Mianus River  16
Morning (For My Father)  48
Mother and Son  9
Mountain Lake View  26
Music Stories  40

**N**

Nine Angels  34
Not Knowing Beauty  43

**P**

Pillow  24
Pomp and Circumstance  22
Post-Communion Buzz  42
Promise  8
Promised Land  55

**R**

Reckoning  3
Rhema  2
Running out of Town  28

**S**

The Swing  35

**T**

The Thrill Is Gone  47
Times Square  50

**W**

Water Balloons  15

# Photographs—
# In Order They Appear

Photograph 1.    Three angles of lattice works skylight and ceiling, Washington, DC

Photograph 2.    Seagulls 1, Outer Banks, North Carolina, and Seagulls 2 over Beach, Outer Banks, North Carolina

Photograph 3.    Bridge at sunset, beach and clouds, beach and bulrushes, Duck, North Carolina

Photograph 4.    Ocean Sunset, Aruba, West Indies; Beach Lagoon, Oahu, Hawaii

Photograph 5.    Sunset over water, clouds, British Virgin Islands

Photograph 6.    Clouds at day, and island clouds in afternoon, US Virgin Islands

Photograph 7.    Four photographs of sea rocks on Virgin Gorda, British Virgin Islands